50 Decadent Chocolate Desserts for Every Occasion

By: Kelly Johnson

Table of Contents

- Chocolate Lava Cake
- Triple Chocolate Brownies
- Dark Chocolate Mousse
- Chocolate Chip Cookies
- Flourless Chocolate Cake
- Chocolate Soufflé
- Chocolate Fudge Brownie Cheesecake
- Chocolate Ganache Tart
- Chocolate Crème Brûlée
- Chocolate Peanut Butter Pie
- Hot Chocolate Pudding
- White Chocolate Raspberry Truffles
- Double Chocolate Chip Muffins
- Chocolate Eclairs
- Chocolate Tiramisu
- Molten Chocolate Bundt Cake
- Chocolate Hazelnut Tart
- Chocolate Cheesecake Bars
- Chocolate-Dipped Strawberries
- Chocolate Bread Pudding
- Chocolate Meringue Pie
- Chocolate Ice Cream Cake
- Chocolate Caramel Tart
- Chocolate Coconut Macaroons
- Chocolate Fondue
- Mexican Hot Chocolate
- Chocolate Babka
- Chocolate Almond Biscotti
- Chocolate Silk Pie
- Chocolate Rum Balls
- Chocolate Mint Brownies
- Chocolate Chiffon Cake
- Chocolate Éclair Cake
- Salted Chocolate Fudge
- Chocolate Croissants

- Chocolate Peanut Butter Cups
- Chocolate Crinkle Cookies
- Chocolate Peanut Butter Fudge
- Chocolate Pecan Pie
- Chocolate Swiss Roll
- Chocolate Raspberry Cake
- Chocolate Pumpkin Tart
- Chocolate Banana Bread
- Chocolate Truffle Cake
- Chocolate Macarons
- Chocolate Dipped Pretzels
- Chocolate Marshmallow Fudge
- Chocolate Breadsticks
- Chocolate Toffee Bark
- Chocolate Peanut Butter Swirl Brownies

Chocolate Lava Cake

Ingredients:

- 4 oz dark chocolate
- ½ cup unsalted butter
- 1 cup powdered sugar
- 2 eggs
- 2 egg yolks
- 6 tbsp all-purpose flour
- 1 tsp vanilla extract
- Pinch of salt

Instructions:

1. **Preheat Oven:** Preheat your oven to 425°F (220°C). Grease and flour 4 ramekins.
2. **Melt Chocolate and Butter:** In a microwave-safe bowl, melt the chocolate and butter together, stirring until smooth.
3. **Mix Ingredients:** Add powdered sugar to the chocolate mixture, then whisk in eggs, egg yolks, vanilla, and salt. Stir in flour until combined.
4. **Bake:** Pour the batter into the prepared ramekins and bake for 12-14 minutes until the edges are firm but the center is soft.
5. **Serve:** Let the cakes cool slightly, then gently run a knife around the edges and invert onto a plate. Serve warm.

Triple Chocolate Brownies

Ingredients:

- ¾ cup unsalted butter, melted
- 1 cup granulated sugar
- 1 cup brown sugar
- 1 cup cocoa powder
- 3 large eggs
- 1 tsp vanilla extract
- 1 cup all-purpose flour
- ½ tsp salt
- ½ cup dark chocolate chips
- ½ cup milk chocolate chips
- ½ cup white chocolate chips

Instructions:

1. **Preheat Oven:** Preheat your oven to 350°F (175°C). Grease an 8x8-inch baking pan.
2. **Make Batter:** In a large bowl, whisk together melted butter, granulated sugar, and brown sugar. Add eggs and vanilla extract, and mix until smooth. Stir in cocoa powder, flour, and salt until combined. Fold in the chocolate chips.
3. **Bake:** Pour the batter into the prepared pan and bake for 30-35 minutes, or until a toothpick comes out with moist crumbs.
4. **Cool and Serve:** Let the brownies cool before slicing and serving.

Dark Chocolate Mousse

Ingredients:

- 6 oz dark chocolate, chopped
- 3 tbsp unsalted butter
- 3 large eggs, separated
- ¼ cup granulated sugar
- 1 cup heavy cream
- 1 tsp vanilla extract
- Pinch of salt

Instructions:

1. **Melt Chocolate and Butter:** In a heatproof bowl, melt dark chocolate and butter together. Let it cool slightly.
2. **Whisk Egg Yolks:** In a small bowl, whisk egg yolks with 2 tbsp sugar until pale. Stir into the chocolate mixture.
3. **Beat Egg Whites:** In another bowl, beat egg whites with the remaining sugar and salt until stiff peaks form.
4. **Whip Cream:** In a separate bowl, whip the heavy cream with vanilla until soft peaks form.
5. **Combine:** Gently fold the egg whites into the chocolate mixture, followed by the whipped cream. Refrigerate for at least 2 hours before serving.

Chocolate Chip Cookies

Ingredients:

- 1 cup unsalted butter, softened
- ¾ cup brown sugar
- ¾ cup granulated sugar
- 2 large eggs
- 1 tsp vanilla extract
- 2 ¼ cups all-purpose flour
- 1 tsp baking soda
- ½ tsp salt
- 2 cups chocolate chips

Instructions:

1. **Preheat Oven:** Preheat your oven to 350°F (175°C). Line a baking sheet with parchment paper.
2. **Make Dough:** Cream together butter, brown sugar, and granulated sugar until fluffy. Add eggs and vanilla and mix until combined. Stir in flour, baking soda, and salt until just combined. Fold in chocolate chips.
3. **Bake:** Drop dough by rounded tablespoons onto the baking sheet. Bake for 10-12 minutes until golden.
4. **Cool and Serve:** Let the cookies cool on the baking sheet for 5 minutes before transferring to a wire rack.

Flourless Chocolate Cake

Ingredients:

- 8 oz dark chocolate, chopped
- ½ cup unsalted butter
- ¾ cup granulated sugar
- 3 large eggs
- ½ cup cocoa powder
- 1 tsp vanilla extract
- Pinch of salt

Instructions:

1. **Preheat Oven:** Preheat your oven to 375°F (190°C). Grease a 9-inch springform pan and line the bottom with parchment paper.
2. **Melt Chocolate and Butter:** In a saucepan, melt chocolate and butter over low heat, stirring until smooth.
3. **Mix Ingredients:** Remove from heat and whisk in sugar, eggs, vanilla, cocoa powder, and salt until smooth.
4. **Bake:** Pour the batter into the prepared pan and bake for 20-25 minutes until the center is set.
5. **Cool and Serve:** Let the cake cool completely before serving, optionally dusted with powdered sugar.

Chocolate Soufflé

Ingredients:

- 4 oz dark chocolate, chopped
- 2 tbsp unsalted butter, plus extra for greasing
- 2 tbsp all-purpose flour
- ¾ cup milk
- 3 large eggs, separated
- ¼ cup granulated sugar
- Pinch of salt
- Powdered sugar for dusting

Instructions:

1. **Preheat Oven:** Preheat oven to 375°F (190°C). Grease ramekins with butter and dust with sugar.
2. **Make Base:** Melt butter in a saucepan, stir in flour, and cook for 1 minute. Gradually whisk in milk and cook until thickened. Remove from heat and stir in chocolate until melted. Let cool.
3. **Mix Eggs:** Stir egg yolks into the chocolate mixture. In a separate bowl, beat egg whites with salt until soft peaks form, then gradually add sugar until stiff peaks form.
4. **Fold and Bake:** Gently fold egg whites into the chocolate mixture. Divide among ramekins and bake for 15-18 minutes until puffed.
5. **Serve:** Dust with powdered sugar and serve immediately.

Chocolate Fudge Brownie Cheesecake

Ingredients:

- 1 ½ cups chocolate cookie crumbs
- ¼ cup melted butter
- 2 cups brownie mix (prepared)
- 16 oz cream cheese, softened
- 1 cup sugar
- 3 large eggs
- 1 tsp vanilla extract
- 1 cup chocolate chips

Instructions:

1. **Preheat Oven:** Preheat oven to 325°F (160°C). Grease a 9-inch springform pan.
2. **Prepare Crust:** Mix cookie crumbs with melted butter and press into the bottom of the pan.
3. **Make Brownie Layer:** Pour prepared brownie batter over the crust and bake for 15 minutes.
4. **Make Cheesecake Layer:** Beat cream cheese with sugar, eggs, and vanilla until smooth. Pour over the brownie layer. Sprinkle with chocolate chips.
5. **Bake:** Bake for 45-50 minutes until the center is set. Let cool completely before refrigerating for at least 4 hours.

Chocolate Ganache Tart

Ingredients:

- 1 ½ cups graham cracker crumbs
- ¼ cup melted butter
- 8 oz dark chocolate, chopped
- 1 cup heavy cream
- 1 tsp vanilla extract

Instructions:

1. **Make Crust:** Mix graham cracker crumbs with melted butter and press into a tart pan. Refrigerate while preparing the filling.
2. **Make Ganache:** In a saucepan, heat the cream until just simmering. Pour over chopped chocolate and let sit for 5 minutes, then stir until smooth.
3. **Assemble and Chill:** Pour the ganache into the prepared crust and refrigerate for at least 2 hours until set.
4. **Serve:** Slice and serve chilled.

Chocolate Crème Brûlée

Ingredients:

- 4 oz dark chocolate
- 2 cups heavy cream
- 5 egg yolks
- ½ cup granulated sugar
- 1 tsp vanilla extract
- ¼ cup sugar (for topping)

Instructions:

1. **Preheat Oven:** Preheat your oven to 325°F (160°C).
2. **Melt Chocolate and Heat Cream:** In a saucepan, heat the cream until just simmering. Remove from heat and add the chocolate, stirring until melted.
3. **Mix Ingredients:** In a bowl, whisk together egg yolks, sugar, and vanilla. Gradually whisk in the chocolate cream mixture.
4. **Bake:** Pour the mixture into ramekins and place them in a baking dish. Fill the dish with hot water halfway up the sides of the ramekins. Bake for 30-35 minutes.
5. **Cool and Caramelize:** Let the custards cool, then refrigerate. Before serving, sprinkle sugar on top and caramelize with a kitchen torch.

Chocolate Peanut Butter Pie

Ingredients:

- 1 ½ cups chocolate cookie crumbs
- ¼ cup melted butter
- 1 cup peanut butter
- 8 oz cream cheese, softened
- 1 cup powdered sugar
- 1 cup whipped cream
- 4 oz chocolate, melted

Instructions:

1. **Make Crust:** Mix cookie crumbs with melted butter and press into a pie dish. Refrigerate while preparing the filling.
2. **Make Filling:** Beat peanut butter, cream cheese, and powdered sugar until smooth. Fold in whipped cream.
3. **Assemble and Chill:** Spread the filling into the crust and drizzle with melted chocolate. Refrigerate for at least 2 hours before serving.

Hot Chocolate Pudding

Ingredients:

- 4 oz dark chocolate, chopped
- 2 cups milk
- ¼ cup sugar
- 2 tbsp cornstarch
- ¼ tsp salt
- 1 tsp vanilla extract

Instructions:

1. **Melt Chocolate:** In a saucepan, melt chocolate with 1 cup of milk over medium heat, stirring until smooth.
2. **Mix Dry Ingredients:** In a small bowl, whisk together sugar, cornstarch, and salt.
3. **Combine:** Add the remaining milk and dry ingredients to the chocolate mixture. Cook over medium heat, stirring constantly, until thickened.
4. **Serve:** Remove from heat, stir in vanilla, and serve warm.

White Chocolate Raspberry Truffles

Ingredients:

- 8 oz white chocolate, chopped
- ¼ cup heavy cream
- ½ cup raspberry preserves
- 1 cup powdered sugar

Instructions:

1. **Melt Chocolate and Heat Cream:** In a saucepan, heat the cream until simmering. Remove from heat and add white chocolate, stirring until smooth.
2. **Mix and Chill:** Stir in raspberry preserves and refrigerate the mixture until firm.
3. **Form Truffles:** Scoop out small amounts of the mixture and roll into balls. Roll in powdered sugar and refrigerate until ready to serve.

Double Chocolate Chip Muffins

Ingredients:

- 1 ½ cups all-purpose flour
- ½ cup cocoa powder
- 1 cup sugar
- 1 tsp baking powder
- ½ tsp baking soda
- ½ tsp salt
- 1 cup milk
- ½ cup vegetable oil
- 1 large egg
- 1 cup chocolate chips

Instructions:

1. **Preheat Oven:** Preheat your oven to 350°F (175°C) and line a muffin tin with paper liners.
2. **Mix Dry Ingredients:** In a large bowl, whisk together flour, cocoa powder, sugar, baking powder, baking soda, and salt.
3. **Combine Wet Ingredients:** In another bowl, whisk together milk, oil, and egg. Add to the dry ingredients and stir until just combined. Fold in chocolate chips.
4. **Bake:** Divide the batter into the muffin tin and bake for 18-20 minutes.

Chocolate Eclairs

Ingredients:

- ½ cup unsalted butter
- 1 cup water
- 1 cup all-purpose flour
- 4 large eggs
- 2 cups pastry cream
- 8 oz dark chocolate, melted

Instructions:

1. **Preheat Oven:** Preheat your oven to 400°F (200°C) and line a baking sheet with parchment paper.
2. **Make Dough:** In a saucepan, bring water and butter to a boil. Remove from heat and stir in flour until it forms a ball. Add eggs, one at a time, until smooth.
3. **Bake:** Pipe the dough onto the baking sheet and bake for 20-25 minutes.
4. **Assemble:** Let the eclairs cool, then fill with pastry cream. Dip the tops in melted chocolate.

Chocolate Tiramisu

Ingredients:

- 8 oz mascarpone cheese
- ½ cup powdered sugar
- 1 cup heavy cream
- ½ cup brewed coffee
- 2 tbsp cocoa powder
- 1 cup chocolate shavings
- 1 package ladyfingers

Instructions:

1. **Make Cream Filling:** Beat mascarpone and powdered sugar until smooth. Whip heavy cream until soft peaks form and fold into the mascarpone mixture.
2. **Dip Ladyfingers:** Dip ladyfingers in coffee and layer in a dish.
3. **Assemble:** Spread the cream mixture over the ladyfingers, dust with cocoa powder, and repeat layers. Top with chocolate shavings and refrigerate for at least 4 hours before serving.

Molten Chocolate Bundt Cake

Ingredients:

- 1 cup butter
- 8 oz dark chocolate, chopped
- 1 ½ cups sugar
- 4 large eggs
- 1 tsp vanilla extract
- 1 cup all-purpose flour
- ½ tsp baking powder
- Pinch of salt

Instructions:

1. **Preheat Oven:** Preheat your oven to 350°F (175°C). Grease and flour a bundt pan.
2. **Melt Chocolate and Butter:** In a saucepan, melt butter and chocolate over low heat, stirring until smooth.
3. **Mix Ingredients:** In a bowl, whisk sugar, eggs, and vanilla. Add the chocolate mixture and stir. Mix in flour, baking powder, and salt.
4. **Bake:** Pour the batter into the bundt pan and bake for 35-40 minutes. Let cool slightly before inverting onto a plate. Serve warm with ice cream.

Chocolate Hazelnut Tart

Ingredients:

- 1 ½ cups hazelnuts, toasted
- 1 cup graham cracker crumbs
- ¼ cup melted butter
- 8 oz dark chocolate
- 1 cup heavy cream
- ¼ cup sugar
- 1 tsp vanilla extract

Instructions:

1. **Make Crust:** Pulse hazelnuts and graham cracker crumbs in a food processor until fine. Add melted butter and press into a tart pan. Chill for 15 minutes.
2. **Make Filling:** Heat the cream and sugar in a saucepan until simmering. Remove from heat and add chocolate, stirring until smooth. Stir in vanilla.
3. **Assemble:** Pour the chocolate filling into the crust and refrigerate until set. Garnish with hazelnuts.

Chocolate Cheesecake Bars

Ingredients:

- 1 ½ cups chocolate cookie crumbs
- ¼ cup melted butter
- 16 oz cream cheese, softened
- ½ cup sugar
- 2 large eggs
- 8 oz dark chocolate, melted
- 1 tsp vanilla extract

Instructions:

1. **Preheat Oven:** Preheat the oven to 325°F (160°C).
2. **Make Crust:** Mix cookie crumbs with melted butter and press into a baking dish.
3. **Make Filling:** Beat cream cheese, sugar, and vanilla until smooth. Add eggs one at a time, then stir in melted chocolate.
4. **Bake:** Pour the filling over the crust and bake for 25-30 minutes. Chill before cutting into bars.

Chocolate-Dipped Strawberries

Ingredients:

- 1 pint fresh strawberries
- 8 oz dark chocolate, chopped
- 1 tbsp coconut oil

Instructions:

1. **Melt Chocolate:** In a double boiler, melt chocolate and coconut oil until smooth.
2. **Dip Strawberries:** Dip each strawberry into the melted chocolate, letting excess drip off.
3. **Chill:** Place the strawberries on parchment paper and refrigerate until the chocolate is set.

Chocolate Bread Pudding

Ingredients:

- 4 cups cubed bread
- 2 cups milk
- ½ cup sugar
- 3 large eggs
- 1 tsp vanilla extract
- 1 cup dark chocolate chips

Instructions:

1. **Preheat Oven:** Preheat your oven to 350°F (175°C).
2. **Make Custard:** In a bowl, whisk together milk, sugar, eggs, and vanilla.
3. **Assemble:** Place the bread cubes in a baking dish and pour the custard over them. Sprinkle with chocolate chips.
4. **Bake:** Bake for 30-35 minutes until the custard is set.

Chocolate Meringue Pie

Ingredients:

- 1 pie crust, pre-baked
- 1 cup sugar
- ½ cup cocoa powder
- ¼ cup cornstarch
- 3 cups milk
- 4 large eggs, separated
- 2 tbsp butter
- 1 tsp vanilla extract
- ½ cup sugar (for meringue)

Instructions:

1. **Make Chocolate Filling:** Whisk together sugar, cocoa, and cornstarch. Gradually add milk and cook over medium heat until thickened. Stir in egg yolks, butter, and vanilla. Pour into the pie crust.
2. **Make Meringue:** Beat egg whites until soft peaks form, then gradually add sugar and beat until stiff peaks form.
3. **Bake:** Spread the meringue over the pie and bake at 350°F (175°C) for 10-12 minutes until golden.

Chocolate Ice Cream Cake

Ingredients:

- 1 quart chocolate ice cream
- 1 quart vanilla ice cream
- 1 ½ cups chocolate cookie crumbs
- ¼ cup melted butter
- 1 cup hot fudge sauce

Instructions:

1. **Make Crust:** Mix cookie crumbs and melted butter, then press into a springform pan. Freeze for 15 minutes.
2. **Layer Ice Cream:** Spread the chocolate ice cream over the crust, then top with vanilla ice cream. Freeze until firm.
3. **Top with Fudge:** Before serving, drizzle hot fudge sauce over the top.

Chocolate Caramel Tart

Ingredients:

- 1 ½ cups all-purpose flour
- ½ cup powdered sugar
- ½ cup butter, chilled
- 2 tbsp cold water
- 1 cup caramel sauce
- 8 oz dark chocolate
- ½ cup heavy cream

Instructions:

1. **Make Crust:** Mix flour, powdered sugar, and butter until crumbly. Add cold water and form a dough. Press into a tart pan and bake at 350°F (175°C) for 15 minutes.
2. **Assemble:** Pour the caramel sauce into the crust.
3. **Make Ganache:** Heat cream and pour over chopped chocolate, stirring until smooth. Pour the chocolate over the caramel and refrigerate until set.

Chocolate Coconut Macaroons

Ingredients:

- 3 cups shredded coconut
- 1 cup sweetened condensed milk
- 1 tsp vanilla extract
- 8 oz dark chocolate, melted

Instructions:

1. **Preheat Oven:** Preheat the oven to 325°F (160°C). Line a baking sheet with parchment paper.
2. **Mix Ingredients:** Combine coconut, sweetened condensed milk, and vanilla in a bowl.
3. **Bake:** Drop spoonfuls onto the baking sheet and bake for 15-18 minutes.
4. **Dip in Chocolate:** Once cooled, dip the bottoms of the macaroons in melted chocolate and let them set on parchment paper.

Chocolate Fondue

Ingredients:

- 8 oz dark chocolate, chopped
- ½ cup heavy cream
- 2 tbsp butter
- 2 tbsp sugar
- 1 tsp vanilla extract
- Assorted fruits, marshmallows, and cookies for dipping

Instructions:

1. **Melt Chocolate:** In a double boiler, melt chocolate with cream, butter, and sugar until smooth. Stir in vanilla extract.
2. **Serve:** Pour into a fondue pot and serve with fruits, marshmallows, and cookies for dipping.

Mexican Hot Chocolate

Ingredients:

- 4 cups milk
- 2 oz dark chocolate, chopped
- 2 tbsp cocoa powder
- 2 tbsp sugar
- 1 tsp cinnamon
- 1 pinch cayenne pepper
- 1 tsp vanilla extract

Instructions:

1. **Heat Milk:** In a saucepan, heat milk until warm.
2. **Add Ingredients:** Whisk in chocolate, cocoa, sugar, cinnamon, cayenne, and vanilla until smooth and frothy. Serve hot.

Chocolate Babka

Ingredients:

- 2 ¾ cups all-purpose flour
- ¼ cup sugar
- 1 tsp salt
- 1 packet instant yeast
- ½ cup milk, warmed
- 2 large eggs
- ¼ cup butter, softened
- 1 cup chocolate spread
- ½ cup chopped walnuts

Instructions:

1. **Make Dough:** Mix flour, sugar, salt, and yeast. Add milk, eggs, and butter to form a dough. Knead until smooth and let rise for 1 hour.
2. **Assemble Babka:** Roll out dough, spread chocolate, and sprinkle with walnuts. Roll up, twist, and place in a loaf pan. Let rise again.
3. **Bake:** Bake at 350°F (175°C) for 35-40 minutes until golden.

Chocolate Almond Biscotti

Ingredients:

- 2 cups all-purpose flour
- ½ cup cocoa powder
- 1 tsp baking powder
- ½ tsp salt
- ¾ cup sugar
- 2 large eggs
- 1 tsp vanilla extract
- ½ cup chopped almonds
- ½ cup chocolate chips

Instructions:

1. **Preheat Oven:** Preheat oven to 350°F (175°C).
2. **Make Dough:** Mix flour, cocoa, baking powder, and salt. Beat eggs, sugar, and vanilla, then stir in dry ingredients, almonds, and chocolate chips.
3. **Bake:** Shape into logs, bake for 25 minutes, then slice and bake again until crisp.

Chocolate Silk Pie

Ingredients:

- 1 pie crust, pre-baked
- 1 cup dark chocolate, melted
- ¾ cup sugar
- ¾ cup butter, softened
- 3 large eggs
- 1 tsp vanilla extract
- Whipped cream for topping

Instructions:

1. **Make Filling:** Beat sugar and butter until light. Gradually add melted chocolate and vanilla. Add eggs one at a time, beating thoroughly.
2. **Assemble Pie:** Pour the filling into the pie crust and chill for at least 4 hours.
3. **Serve:** Top with whipped cream before serving.

Chocolate Rum Balls

Ingredients:

- 1 ½ cups crushed chocolate wafers
- ½ cup powdered sugar
- ¼ cup cocoa powder
- ¼ cup dark rum
- 2 tbsp corn syrup
- ½ cup finely chopped nuts
- Sprinkles or cocoa powder for coating

Instructions:

1. **Mix Ingredients:** In a bowl, combine crushed wafers, powdered sugar, cocoa, rum, corn syrup, and nuts until it forms a dough.
2. **Shape Balls:** Roll dough into small balls, then roll in sprinkles or cocoa powder.
3. **Chill:** Refrigerate until firm.

Chocolate Mint Brownies

Ingredients:

- 1 cup butter
- 8 oz dark chocolate
- 1 ½ cups sugar
- 4 large eggs
- 1 tsp vanilla extract
- 1 cup flour
- ½ tsp salt
- 1 tsp peppermint extract
- 1 cup chocolate chips

Instructions:

1. **Preheat Oven:** Preheat oven to 350°F (175°C).
2. **Melt Chocolate:** Melt butter and chocolate together. Stir in sugar, eggs, vanilla, and peppermint.
3. **Bake:** Mix in flour, salt, and chocolate chips. Pour into a baking dish and bake for 25-30 minutes until set.

Chocolate Chiffon Cake

Ingredients:

- 1 ¾ cups all-purpose flour
- ¼ cup cocoa powder
- 1 ½ cups sugar
- 1 tsp baking powder
- ½ tsp salt
- ½ cup vegetable oil
- 7 large eggs, separated
- ¾ cup water
- 1 tsp vanilla extract

Instructions:

1. **Preheat Oven:** Preheat oven to 325°F (160°C).
2. **Mix Batter:** Sift flour, cocoa, sugar, baking powder, and salt. In another bowl, beat egg yolks, oil, water, and vanilla, then combine with dry ingredients.
3. **Whip Egg Whites:** Beat egg whites until stiff, then fold into the batter.
4. **Bake:** Pour into an ungreased tube pan and bake for 50-55 minutes. Cool upside down.

Chocolate Éclair Cake

Ingredients:

- 2 packs of instant vanilla pudding
- 3 cups milk
- 1 container whipped topping
- 1 box graham crackers
- 1 ½ cups chocolate frosting

Instructions:

1. **Prepare Pudding:** Whisk pudding mix with milk until thick, then fold in whipped topping.
2. **Layer:** In a baking dish, layer graham crackers, pudding mix, and repeat. Top with graham crackers.
3. **Frost:** Spread chocolate frosting on top. Chill for 4 hours before serving.

Salted Chocolate Fudge

Ingredients:

- 1 can sweetened condensed milk
- 2 cups dark chocolate chips
- 1 tsp vanilla extract
- 1 tsp sea salt

Instructions:

1. **Melt Chocolate:** In a saucepan, melt chocolate with condensed milk. Stir in vanilla.
2. **Set Fudge:** Pour into a lined dish, sprinkle with sea salt, and refrigerate until firm. Cut into squares.

Chocolate Croissants

Ingredients:

- 1 pack puff pastry sheets
- ½ cup chocolate chips
- 1 egg, beaten
- Powdered sugar for dusting

Instructions:

1. **Preheat Oven:** Preheat oven to 375°F (190°C).
2. **Assemble Croissants:** Cut puff pastry into triangles. Place chocolate chips in the center and roll up. Brush with egg wash.
3. **Bake:** Bake for 15-20 minutes until golden. Dust with powdered sugar before serving.

Chocolate Peanut Butter Cups

Ingredients:

- 2 cups dark chocolate, melted
- ½ cup peanut butter
- 2 tbsp powdered sugar
- 1 tbsp butter

Instructions:

1. **Prepare Filling:** Mix peanut butter, powdered sugar, and butter until smooth.
2. **Assemble Cups:** Pour melted chocolate into mini muffin liners, add a dollop of peanut butter mix, and top with more chocolate.
3. **Chill:** Refrigerate until set.

Chocolate Crinkle Cookies

Ingredients:

- 1 cup cocoa powder
- 2 cups sugar
- ½ cup vegetable oil
- 4 large eggs
- 2 tsp vanilla extract
- 2 cups all-purpose flour
- 2 tsp baking powder
- ½ tsp salt
- Powdered sugar for rolling

Instructions:

1. **Make Dough:** Mix cocoa, sugar, and oil. Beat in eggs and vanilla. Stir in flour, baking powder, and salt.
2. **Chill Dough:** Chill dough for 1 hour.
3. **Bake:** Roll dough into balls, coat in powdered sugar, and bake at 350°F (175°C) for 10-12 minutes.

Chocolate Peanut Butter Fudge

Ingredients:

- 2 cups sugar
- ½ cup milk
- ¾ cup peanut butter
- 1 tsp vanilla extract
- ½ cup cocoa powder

Instructions:

1. **Heat Mixture:** Bring sugar, milk, and cocoa to a boil. Cook for 5 minutes.
2. **Add Peanut Butter:** Remove from heat, stir in peanut butter and vanilla.
3. **Set Fudge:** Pour into a dish and let cool before cutting.

Chocolate Pecan Pie

Ingredients:

- 1 pie crust
- 1 cup corn syrup
- ½ cup sugar
- 3 large eggs
- 2 tbsp butter, melted
- 1 tsp vanilla extract
- 1 cup pecans
- ½ cup chocolate chips

Instructions:

1. **Preheat Oven:** Preheat oven to 350°F (175°C).
2. **Prepare Filling:** Mix corn syrup, sugar, eggs, butter, and vanilla. Stir in pecans and chocolate chips.
3. **Bake:** Pour into pie crust and bake for 50-55 minutes until set.

Chocolate Swiss Roll

Ingredients:

- 4 large eggs
- ¾ cup sugar
- ¾ cup flour
- ¼ cup cocoa powder
- 1 tsp baking powder
- 2 tbsp melted butter
- Whipped cream for filling
- Powdered sugar for dusting

Instructions:

1. **Preheat Oven:** Preheat oven to 350°F (175°C).
2. **Make Batter:** Beat eggs and sugar until fluffy. Sift in flour, cocoa, and baking powder. Fold in melted butter.
3. **Bake:** Pour batter into a lined baking sheet and bake for 10-12 minutes.
4. **Assemble Roll:** Spread whipped cream on the cake and roll it up. Dust with powdered sugar.

Chocolate Raspberry Cake

Ingredients:

- 1 ¾ cups all-purpose flour
- 1 ¾ cups sugar
- ¾ cup unsweetened cocoa powder
- 1 ½ tsp baking powder
- 1 ½ tsp baking soda
- 1 tsp salt
- 2 large eggs
- 1 cup whole milk
- ½ cup vegetable oil
- 2 tsp vanilla extract
- 1 cup boiling water
- 1 cup fresh raspberries
- Chocolate ganache for frosting

Instructions:

1. **Preheat Oven:** Preheat the oven to 350°F (175°C). Grease and flour two 9-inch round cake pans.
2. **Mix Dry Ingredients:** In a large bowl, combine flour, sugar, cocoa, baking powder, baking soda, and salt.
3. **Add Wet Ingredients:** Add eggs, milk, oil, and vanilla. Beat for 2 minutes. Stir in boiling water until smooth.
4. **Bake:** Divide the batter between the prepared pans. Bake for 30-35 minutes. Cool completely.
5. **Assemble Cake:** Layer cakes with chocolate ganache and fresh raspberries. Frost the top and sides with ganache.

Chocolate Pumpkin Tart

Ingredients:

- 1 pre-made pie crust
- 1 cup pumpkin puree
- ½ cup sugar
- ½ cup heavy cream
- 2 large eggs
- ½ cup unsweetened cocoa powder
- 1 tsp vanilla extract
- ½ tsp pumpkin pie spice
- Pinch of salt

Instructions:

1. **Preheat Oven:** Preheat the oven to 350°F (175°C).
2. **Prepare Filling:** In a bowl, whisk together pumpkin puree, sugar, heavy cream, eggs, cocoa powder, vanilla, pumpkin pie spice, and salt until smooth.
3. **Bake Tart:** Pour the filling into the pie crust and bake for 45-50 minutes, or until set.
4. **Cool and Serve:** Allow to cool completely before slicing. Serve with whipped cream if desired.

Chocolate Banana Bread

Ingredients:

- 2-3 ripe bananas, mashed
- ½ cup unsalted butter, melted
- 1 cup sugar
- 2 large eggs
- 1 tsp vanilla extract
- 1 tsp baking soda
- ¼ tsp salt
- 1 ½ cups all-purpose flour
- ½ cup chocolate chips

Instructions:

1. **Preheat Oven:** Preheat the oven to 350°F (175°C). Grease a 9x5-inch loaf pan.
2. **Mix Wet Ingredients:** In a bowl, mix mashed bananas, melted butter, sugar, eggs, and vanilla until combined.
3. **Add Dry Ingredients:** Stir in baking soda and salt, then mix in flour until just combined. Fold in chocolate chips.
4. **Bake:** Pour the batter into the prepared pan and bake for 60-65 minutes, or until a toothpick comes out clean. Cool before slicing.

Chocolate Truffle Cake

Ingredients:

- 8 oz bittersweet chocolate, chopped
- ½ cup unsalted butter
- ¾ cup sugar
- 3 large eggs
- 1 tsp vanilla extract
- 1 cup all-purpose flour
- Cocoa powder for dusting

Instructions:

1. **Preheat Oven:** Preheat the oven to 350°F (175°C). Grease a 9-inch round cake pan.
2. **Melt Chocolate:** In a double boiler, melt chocolate and butter until smooth.
3. **Combine Ingredients:** Remove from heat, whisk in sugar, then add eggs one at a time. Stir in vanilla and flour until just combined.
4. **Bake:** Pour the batter into the prepared pan and bake for 25-30 minutes.
5. **Cool and Serve:** Let cool completely, dust with cocoa powder, and serve with whipped cream if desired.

Chocolate Macarons

Ingredients:

- 1 cup powdered sugar
- ½ cup almond flour
- 3 large egg whites
- ¼ cup granulated sugar
- 1 tsp vanilla extract
- 2 tbsp unsweetened cocoa powder
- Chocolate ganache for filling

Instructions:

1. **Preheat Oven:** Preheat the oven to 300°F (150°C) and line baking sheets with parchment paper.
2. **Mix Dry Ingredients:** In a bowl, sift together powdered sugar, almond flour, and cocoa powder.
3. **Whip Egg Whites:** In a separate bowl, beat egg whites until foamy. Gradually add granulated sugar and beat until stiff peaks form.
4. **Combine Mixtures:** Gently fold the dry ingredients into the egg whites until fully combined.
5. **Pipe Macarons:** Pipe small circles onto prepared baking sheets. Let them rest for 30 minutes to form a skin.
6. **Bake:** Bake for 15-20 minutes. Cool completely before filling with chocolate ganache.

Chocolate Dipped Pretzels

Ingredients:

- 1 cup chocolate chips (milk or dark chocolate)
- 1 cup pretzel rods or mini pretzels
- Sprinkles or crushed nuts (optional)

Instructions:

1. **Melt Chocolate:** In a microwave-safe bowl, melt the chocolate chips in 30-second intervals, stirring in between until smooth.
2. **Dip Pretzels:** Dip each pretzel rod or mini pretzel halfway into the melted chocolate, letting the excess drip off.
3. **Add Toppings:** If desired, sprinkle with toppings like sprinkles or crushed nuts before the chocolate sets.
4. **Cool:** Place the dipped pretzels on a baking sheet lined with parchment paper. Refrigerate until the chocolate hardens.
5. **Serve:** Enjoy as a sweet and salty snack!

Chocolate Marshmallow Fudge

Ingredients:

- 2 cups semi-sweet chocolate chips
- 1 can (14 oz) sweetened condensed milk
- 1 tsp vanilla extract
- 1 cup mini marshmallows
- ¼ cup chopped nuts (optional)

Instructions:

1. **Prepare Pan:** Line an 8x8-inch baking dish with parchment paper.
2. **Melt Chocolate:** In a saucepan over low heat, combine chocolate chips and sweetened condensed milk. Stir until melted and smooth.
3. **Add Ingredients:** Remove from heat, stir in vanilla, mini marshmallows, and nuts if using.
4. **Pour and Chill:** Pour the fudge mixture into the prepared pan and spread evenly. Refrigerate for at least 2 hours or until firm.
5. **Cut and Serve:** Lift out of the pan, cut into squares, and serve.

Chocolate Breadsticks

Ingredients:

- 1 package (1 lb) pizza dough (store-bought or homemade)
- ½ cup chocolate chips
- 1 tbsp butter, melted
- 2 tbsp powdered sugar
- Sea salt (optional)

Instructions:

1. **Preheat Oven:** Preheat the oven to 425°F (220°C).
2. **Prepare Dough:** Roll out the pizza dough into a rectangle and cut into strips about ½ inch wide.
3. **Shape Breadsticks:** Twist each strip to form a breadstick shape. Place them on a baking sheet lined with parchment paper.
4. **Bake:** Bake for 10-12 minutes or until golden brown.
5. **Melt Chocolate:** In a microwave-safe bowl, melt the chocolate chips and butter together until smooth.
6. **Dip and Serve:** Drizzle melted chocolate over the warm breadsticks or dip them in chocolate. Sprinkle with powdered sugar or sea salt if desired.

Chocolate Toffee Bark

Ingredients:

- 1 cup butter
- 1 cup brown sugar
- 2 cups chocolate chips (milk or semi-sweet)
- 1 cup chopped nuts (almonds, walnuts, or pecans)

Instructions:

1. **Preheat Oven:** Preheat the oven to 350°F (175°C). Line a baking sheet with foil or parchment paper.
2. **Make Toffee:** In a saucepan, melt butter and brown sugar over medium heat. Bring to a boil, stirring constantly for 3-4 minutes until thickened.
3. **Spread Mixture:** Pour the toffee mixture onto the prepared baking sheet and spread evenly.
4. **Bake:** Bake in the oven for 10-12 minutes until bubbly.
5. **Add Chocolate:** Remove from the oven and immediately sprinkle chocolate chips on top. Let sit for a few minutes until melted, then spread the chocolate evenly.
6. **Add Nuts:** Sprinkle chopped nuts over the chocolate, pressing down gently.
7. **Cool and Break:** Allow to cool completely at room temperature or refrigerate. Once set, break into pieces and serve.

Chocolate Peanut Butter Swirl Brownies

Ingredients:

- 1 cup unsalted butter
- 2 cups sugar
- 4 large eggs
- 1 tsp vanilla extract
- 1 cup all-purpose flour
- 1 cup unsweetened cocoa powder
- ½ tsp salt
- 1 cup creamy peanut butter

Instructions:

1. **Preheat Oven:** Preheat the oven to 350°F (175°C). Grease a 9x13-inch baking pan.
2. **Melt Butter:** In a saucepan, melt butter over low heat. Remove from heat and stir in sugar, eggs, and vanilla.
3. **Mix Dry Ingredients:** In a separate bowl, combine flour, cocoa powder, and salt. Gradually add to the wet mixture until combined.
4. **Add Peanut Butter:** Pour half the brownie batter into the prepared pan. In a small bowl, microwave peanut butter until melted, then drizzle it over the brownie batter.
5. **Swirl Mixture:** Add the remaining brownie batter on top and use a knife to swirl the peanut butter into the batter.
6. **Bake:** Bake for 25-30 minutes or until a toothpick comes out with a few moist crumbs.
7. **Cool and Cut:** Allow to cool before cutting into squares and serving.

www.ingramcontent.com/pod-product-compliance
Lightning Source LLC
LaVergne TN
LVHW081335060526
838201LV00055B/2657